DEAR Young MISS

Ms. Joyce

ISBN 979-8-89428-007-3 (paperback)
ISBN 979-8-89428-008-0 (digital)

Christian Faith Publishing
832 Park Avenue
Meadville, PA 16335
www.christianfaithpublishing.com

Images from Shutterstock.com

Printed in the United States of America

To Marcus and Katrina, forever in my heart

Will you become part of the next thinking generation (NTG)?

You might find this a strange question to ask. However, if you read this book, you will understand what I mean. I can start by saying that as females, we take a similar biological path as we grow and age. In other words, our bodies change and develop when we start experiencing puberty. We usually grow much taller, and our body shapes change. We are all different. For me, I stopped growing in height when I was around twelve years old. I am five feet and two inches tall. I don't mind being short. If I want to reach something on a high shelf, I will ask for help or get a stool. Nobody has ever refused to help me. When I was growing up, I was very slender. As a teenager, I started drinking milkshakes all the time because someone had told me that it would help me gain weight. I wanted to be larger because other girls looked more mature than me. After a while, I stopped taking the advice about drinking milkshakes because I didn't see any difference in my weight. Plus, I decided that my size was perfect. Now I also realize when looking back that just through aging, our body shapes can change with added weight. I have found that the key for me has been to monitor what types of food I eat, drink plenty of water, and exercise.

The word *puberty* is defined as a length of time when a girl's body goes through physical changes that allow her to reproduce. This means she can have a baby. Puberty is the time when girls get hair over their genitals. Their ovaries, fallopian tubes, and uterus become center stage. The uterus, ovaries, and fallopian tubes all play a role when a girl starts to have a menstrual cycle, or period. What is a menstrual period, and what is its purpose? Menstruation, or period, is normal vaginal bleeding that occurs as part of a woman's monthly cycle. Every month your body prepares for pregnancy. If no pregnancy occurs, the uterus or womb sheds its lining. The menstrual blood is partly blood and partly tissue from inside the uterus. It passes out of the body through the vagina.[1]

As stated previously, the purpose of a menstrual cycle is to reproduce. This can happen when a female has sexual intercourse with a male. If an egg from the female ovary and a sperm cell from a male unite during intercourse, the result could be the conception of a fertilized egg. When a sperm and egg unite, the conception is the beginning of a life. The fertilized egg is genetically endowed with forty-six chromosomes: twenty-three from the biological father and twenty-three from the biological mother.[2]

Chromosomes play a key role in determining the baby's sex and physical traits. This is how your life began—with the conception of an egg and sperm that occurred in one of your mother's fallopian tubes. The fertilized cell builds momentum by becoming a cluster of cells and then embeds, or plants, itself in the uterus of the mother.[3] An interesting point is that even though life begins at conception, time is required for the baby to develop in the mother's womb, or uterus. The baby's arrival date is calculated from the start date of a female's last period, counting forward forty weeks.[4] It seems like there are sometimes exceptions to the rule, but normally, babies are born around their time.

---

[1] https://www.MedlinePlus.gov.

[2] https://www.Mayoclinic.org/healthy-lifestyle/pregnancy-week-by-week/basics/healthy.

[3] https://www.Mayoclinic.org/healthy-lifestyle/pregnancy-week-by-week/basics/healthy.

[4] https://www.Mayoclinic.org.

Periods usually begin in a cycle every twenty-one to thirty-five days[5] when the lining inside the uterus sloughs off, which means it detaches from the uterus and flows out through the vagina in its own sympatric rhythm. This calls for purchasing and wearing protection to keep from soiling underwear during this process. Young girls differ in their experiences during this time period. The occurrence of a menstrual period varies, with its start anytime between the ages of nine and fifteen.[6] Some girls have mood swings, stomach cramps, bloating, tiredness, sore breasts, aches in their body, and so forth. On the other hand, some girls have little or no known symptoms of pain. When I was a girl, I remember experiencing achiness in my legs, stomach cramps, and breast tenderness. When this happened to me, I would just curl up in my bed and sleep because the cramps hurt for a day or two. I still went to school and engaged in other activities. I don't recall missing school days because of my period. I probably wanted to stay home at times but didn't want to get behind in my schoolwork. My teachers loaded us up with homework too.

Sometimes, as the lining of the uterus passes through the vagina, the bleeding may be more intense the first three days, then tapers off until it is gone. An example is turning off a faucet of drizzling water that suddenly comes on again in the next twenty-one to thirty-five days. Keep in mind that the length of a period also varies among girls. It could last between three to seven days.[7]

Your experience as you start having a menstrual period will be unique to you, even though this biological cycle is what females have in common. An array of differences will occur in girls concerning their thinking about this biological cycle depending on how they view their bodies and themselves. By this, I mean that some girls may think that they never want to have a baby. Some may just hate the monthly process. Others may look forward to meeting the right man and having a family. Nevertheless, this is a phenomenon that only

---

[5]   https://www.YoungWomen'sHealth.org.

[6]   https://www.YoungWomen'sHealth.org.

[7]   https://www.YoungWomen'sHealth.org.

biological females share that makes us collectively a part of the circle of womanhood.

As a girl grows up around the age of ten and upward, she may start to have special feelings for a boy where they might kiss and touch each other in private places on their bodies. This could lead to the pair joining in mutual sexual intercourse and the girl possibly becoming pregnant. Before sexual intercourse happens, however, a girl should think seriously about her actions.

She should ask herself several questions and think deeply about each one of them. Here are some suggestions.

The first question is, why do I want to have sex with this particular boy?

____

____

____

How would I feel if I find out that I am pregnant?

____

____

____

How do I think he will respond if I tell him that I am pregnant?

____

____

____

If I get pregnant, who will take care of the baby? Why?

____

____

____

Would this boy make a good father? Explain.

____

____

____

Would he get a job when he is of age and help take care of his child?

____

____

____

Do I love him? Why or why not?

____

____

____

Does he love me? Give different examples of how you know.

____

____

____

Does he respect me? In what ways does he show respect?

____

____

____

Do I think that he will make a good role model for his child?

____

____

____

Here are some other questions to consider.
Will he make a good marriage mate?

____

____

____

Do I see myself with him ten years from now? Explain your answer.

____

____

____

Do I think that I will still like him when we are both ten years older?

____

____

____

Does he only say nice things to my face, or does he criticize and talk down to me at times?

____

____

____

Do my close friends like him? Why or why not?

____

____

____

Do my parents know him? What do they think about him?

____

____

____

Do my parents like him? Why or why not?

____

____

____

Do I know his family? How do they talk to him? How does he talk to them?

____

____

____

Do they like me? How do I know? Do I like them?

____

____

____

Consider that getting pregnant and having a baby with this boy will bind, or join, you to him for the rest of your life. Do you want that kind of long-term connection with him?

____

____

____

What do you like about this boy now? List responses.

____

____

____

What does he want to do as a career?

____

____

____

Is he preparing for a career now and talking like it's a real goal that he plans to achieve?

____

____

____

Is he learning, studying, and paying attention in school now?

____

____

____

Are you staying focused on your schoolwork now?

____

____

____

What are your academic goals for high school graduation? Do you want to find a particular type of job, attend a vocational or technical school, or go to a university and graduate?

Asking yourself these questions and more can help you think deeply about what kind of person you want in your life as you move forward into your future. You should ask yourself if attraction to each other is enough.

If you get pregnant, do you expect to marry this boy and that the two of you will take care of the child together?

Think about the cost of your getting pregnant at an early or young age. Do you want to physically take care of a baby (i.e., feed them, bathe them, clothe them, love them, and take care of them if they are sick)?

Think about spending time to play with the child and committing to teaching the child social skills so that they are prepared to interact peacefully with others in an academic or social environment. Are you willing to do this for the child?

Will you love the child if it looks like a boy who is no longer in your life?

____

____

____

Do you expect your mother to take care of the child for extended periods of time?

____

____

____

If this is your expectation, what do you think your mother will say about adding this type of responsibility to her life?

____

____

____

The last question remains, and that is, if you are not ready to fully commit to loving and taking care of a baby yourself, then why would you have sexual intercourse with this boy?

____

____

____

Think deeply about the delays it will cause in your life and the impact it will have on the goals you set for your future.

You could say that you and the boy will be careful so that you won't get pregnant. Many babies have been born despite that reasoning. Let's say that you do decide to have sex and get pregnant unintentionally. What now?

____

____

____

I have read interesting details about what happens during a pregnancy. I didn't know all these things when I got pregnant as a married adult. I want to share some of the information with you now.

Every person alive on this earth has experienced the logical order of the building process of a pregnancy. If a girl has sexual intercourse with a boy, one of the first alerts that she could be pregnant is that her menstrual periods stop. Having nausea could also be another alert to a possible pregnancy. A pregnancy can be confirmed with a test. Seeing a positive reading on a pregnancy test is a very exciting thing for a woman who wants a baby. A pregnant female can expect a lot of activity to occur inside her body during the first trimester, or three months. The fertilized egg, now a cluster of cells, has embedded, or planted, itself in the uterus, becoming more detailed in structure, consisting of three layers with a purpose. The outer layer will form the skin, eyes, and inner ear, as well as the central and peripheral nervous systems. The middle layer will form the heart and circulatory system and give rise to the developing bones, kidneys, ligaments, and reproductive system. The inner layer orchestrates the development of the baby's lungs and intestines. The brain and spinal cord will develop from a neural tube along the baby's back. Arms and legs start to form. The head, brain, body, heart, lungs, intestines, and other organs are developing during this time. The face, ears, and external genitalia (the indicator of the sex of the baby) are starting to develop.[8] In essence, the baby's parts are all being assembled. Ten weeks after conception, the baby is growing fingernails.[9] All of this happens within the first three months of pregnancy.

During the second trimester of pregnancy (the fourth, fifth, and sixth months), the baby is growing swiftly. The baby can release urine into the amniotic sac. The baby's skeleton starts to harden. The scalp's hair pattern is taking shape, and the baby's limbs and eyes

---

[8] https://www.MayoClinic.org/healthy-lifestyle/pregnancy-week-by-week/basics/healthy.

[9] https://www.MayoClinic.org/healthy-lifestyle/pregnancy-week-by-week/basics/healthy.

move.[10] As you can see, a lot of activity is happening inside a female's body during pregnancy.

In addition, a baby girl's uterus and vaginal canal are taking shape. Hair and eyebrows can be seen. A baby boy's testes are beginning to descend. The baby will roll and flip inside the amniotic sac. The baby might get hiccups, which causes jerking movements. The baby's hearing might allow it to respond to its mother's voice.[11] How? By movement. In the second trimester of pregnancy, the baby is putting on weight.

During the third trimester of pregnancy (the seventh, eighth, and ninth months), the baby has eyelashes and can open its eyes wide.[12] The baby can kick, stretch, wiggle, and roll, just as your mother can tell you from when you were inside her body! The majority of the development of the baby has occurred twenty-nine weeks after conception. Toenails and fingernails grow to the tips of toes and fingers, and the baby adds that fat to the body, which is a hallmark of how they look when they are born.[13]

You can liken a pregnancy to going on a road trip in a vehicle. Let's say that on the road trip, it takes a total of three hours to get to your destination. During the first hour of traveling, you know that you are moving forward in the vehicle because you can look out the windows and see different sites, such as other vehicles, motorists, buildings, trees, and road markers that alert you to what is ahead, like places to eat and where to purchase gasoline. Inside your vehicle, you might play games for a while, text or talk on your cell phone, or fall asleep to pass the time.

Let's say that you stop because someone driving the vehicle wants to purchase more gasoline. You notice that one hour has passed. Think of the activities that have occurred inside the vehicle as you traveled in the first hour. This is the same scenario during the

---

[10] https.www.MayoClinic.org/healthy-lifestyle/pregnancy-week-by-week/basics/healthy.

[11] https.www.MayoClinic.org.

[12] https.www.MayoClinic.org.

[13] https.www.MayoClinic.org.

first trimester, or three months, of a pregnancy. Things are happening inside the female's body. Because conception has occurred, the process of the baby's development is underway with a destination too. It's just like you beginning this road trip; you are on your way to a destination.

In your second hour of traveling in your vehicle, you may talk about different topics with your family or play the next level or chapter of a video game. You are aware that the vehicle is moving forward to the same destination. You might add some other activities to occupy your time during this second hour of travel. Likewise, with the second trimester (the fourth, fifth, and sixth months) of a pregnancy, additional building activities are occurring inside the female's body that add to the development of a baby, leading to its own uniqueness as a person.

While you are traveling in your vehicle, functions are occurring in your body that you do not realize until you have to stop off the road at a restaurant or maybe a gasoline station to go to the bathroom to eliminate urine. During the second trimester of pregnancy, the development or functions that occur in the baby proceed effortlessly without the expectant mother having to make these functions happen herself, just like how going to the bathroom to urinate is usually a function that happens effortlessly. When you stop to go to the bathroom, you look at your cell phone and notice that two hours have passed. Now you have only one more hour to go until you arrive at your destination.

Now the three-hour road trip has come to an end. You have reached your destination. You are standing outside the vehicle, ready to enjoy a vacation. Think about it. The same thing occurs with a baby. It reaches its destination of being ready to move forward to the outside world by going through its mother's birth canal, or vagina, on, before, or after its calculated due date. As a baby moves to the outside world, it has the opportunity to enjoy its life. It starts with the baby being greeted by a mother who welcomes it into the world. As you can see from this description of a road trip and its comparison with the progression of a baby's development, nothing stops the baby's progress to enjoy personhood. You didn't change your mind about going on the road trip. The development of a baby does not stop until it reaches its destination unless the mother has a miscarriage.

A miscarriage, according to *Merriam-Webster Dictionary*, is "a spontaneous expulsion of a human fetus before it is viable, especially between the 12th and 28th weeks of gestation."[14] Another definition is "a condition in which a pregnancy ends too early and does not result in the birth of a live baby."[15]

I know about "spontaneous expulsions." I had two miscarriages, one at five months and another at six months. The first baby was a boy, and the second baby was a girl. The miscarriages happened decades ago, but I remember vividly the losses with horrific pain. My children were given names, Marcus and Katrina, in anticipation of their births. I could see at Marcus's premature birth that his face looked just like his father's. Katrina had a round-shaped face like mine. She lived for one hour. Because of that fact, I arranged a funeral for her. Some of the people from my job left work to attend the graveside funeral. I didn't know that I could cry so uncontrollably. It was one of the saddest days of my life. I had my hopes up that this time was going to have a different outcome, and I would have a baby to hold in my arms. It was hard going through those miserable experiences as a want-to-be mother.

At the time of the losses, I wondered if I had done something wrong. Those thoughts kept going through my mind for a very long time. Remembering back, I knew that I had eaten properly, taken my prenatal vitamins, and went to every doctor appointment. I didn't smoke, I didn't drink alcoholic beverages, and so forth. It was a time of feeling very powerless and sad and thinking that life just wasn't fair. Some people even started telling me that I should just give up. I thought about it, but over time, I found out that I was strong enough not to listen to those voices. However, I wondered how something innate for females as having a baby was so difficult for me to achieve personally.

---

[14] http://www.Merriam-Webster.com.
[15] https://languages.oup.com/dictionaries/english-language-learners/.

Aside from a miscarriage, another way that a baby does not reach its destination is through an abortion.

> An abortion is a procedure to end a pregnancy; it
> uses medicine or surgery to remove the embryo
> or fetus and placenta from the uterus.[16]

According to *Merriam-Webster Dictionary*, the word *medicine* is defined as "a substance or preparation used in treating disease; something that affects well-being: a substance (such as a drug or potion) used to treat something other than disease."[17]

What type of medicine do you think is being used in the procedure of abortion?

____

____

____

Do you think that the medicine is being used to heal or harm?

____

____

____

What type of surgery is being performed by a doctor to remove the embryo, or fetus, or baby, out of the mother's body?

____

____

____

So far, in the United States of America, there have been 63,036,733 abortions since 1973.[18] There are different reasons some women choose to have abortions. Over 90 percent have been by women who decided not to continue the pregnancy after voluntarily

---

[16] https: www.MedlinePlus.gov.

[17] https.//www.Meriam-Webster.com.

[18] https//www.NumberofAbortions.com (as of August 14, 2021; website data).

allowing conception to occur through sexual intercourse with a male. Around 6 percent of abortions were for young girls whose parents wanted the terminations, 1 percent were victims of rape, and less than 0.5 percent were terminated because of incest.[19] *Incest* is defined as "sexual relations between people classed as being too closely related to marry each other, the crime of having sexual intercourse with a parent, child, sibling, or grandchild."[20]

If a girl finds herself being touched on the private parts of her body by a relative (e.g., an uncle or male cousin), then she should tell someone that she trusts about what has happened to her. She needs to do this as early as possible before it occurs again so that she can feel safe. It is possible that a mother might not believe her daughter if the offender is her husband or boyfriend. A girl might also become so afraid that she is too scared to tell anyone, especially if the offender threatens her to keep her mouth shut. In this case, the girl should consider telling someone outside of her home—like a trusted relative, teacher, or school counselor; a good friend's parent; a pastor's wife; a pastor; or a youth religious leader—or seek legal authority, such as a police officer. It is definitely a fearful situation when a girl doesn't know what will happen to her in this type of circumstance, but she can't allow herself to be so scared that she does nothing. She must have courage and realize that nobody has a right to take advantage of her by abusing her body and damaging her emotionally.

If you found yourself in this type of situation, what would you do?

____

____

____

Who would you talk to?

____

____

____

---

[19] https.www.NumberofAbortions.com (as of August 14, 2021; website data).
[20] https.www.Lexico.com.

Another definition for *abortion* says that it "is the deliberate termination of a human pregnancy, most often performed during the first 28 weeks of pregnancy."[21] In regard to the 63,036,733 abortions that have been done since 1973 in the United States, you can see from the numbers that most abortions have occurred because the women did not want to continue the pregnancy.

Do you think it is important to seriously think about whether you want a baby before having sex with someone?

____

____

____

Merriam-Webster Dictionary gives this definition of birth control: "Control of the number of children or offspring born especially by preventing or lessening the frequency of conception: contraceptive devices or preparations."[22]

Do you think it is necessary to talk to your doctor about the various birth control methods and contraceptives available?

____

____

____

Birth control should not be one-sided. There is birth control for men. If you aren't ready to have a baby, then a mutual discussion should ensue between you and the man. Find out if he is willing to use birth control. If he is nonchalant or indifferent about the matter, is he the right fit for you?

____

____

____

---

21 https://www.Lexico.com.

22 https://www.Merriam-Webster.com.

Do you think that aborting a baby is a birth control method? Why or why not?

The research shows that one reason some women have abortions is that their boyfriend didn't want the child.[23] Therefore, do you think that it is necessary to find out if the male wants to have children?

Would you have an abortion because the father didn't want the baby?

Finding out how a man thinks before becoming sexually involved with him is very important. Unfortunately, there have been incidents of physical harm brought to some women for conceiving a child by a man that was vehemently opposed to the prospect of fatherhood. It is helpful to pay attention to your female intuition. It is a quick insight deep down inside you without anyone else telling you what to think. That quick insight should not be ignored. An example is going ahead and doing something and later saying to yourself, "Something told me not to do that."

Have you ever had that experience?

---

[23] https://www.NumberofAbortions.com.

This could apply to becoming involved with someone, but your initial instincts or female intuition told you to get away from that person. Listening to that voice inside ourselves can save the circle of womanhood much heartache and pain.

What should a woman do to avoid such encounters?

____

____

____

As a young girl, you are already a part of the next thinking generation (NTG). Unlike previous female ancestors, please take the time to think ahead about whether you want a baby and are willing to love and take care of a child. Some young women have fallen prey to one-sided propaganda that glamorizes sex, parties, meeting that cute guy, and having one sexual night or a more amazing relationship with an individual that later proves to be a disappointment, leaving the girl pregnant and alone. This is a definition of *propaganda*: "The spreading of ideas, information, or rumor for the purpose of helping or injuring an institution, a cause, or a person."[24]

What if women thought more highly of themselves, not allowing men to dominate their bodies and becoming more selective about who and what they expect in a relationship?

____

____

____

Do you believe such meditation or deep thinking would reduce the number of women seeking abortions?

____

____

____

No doubt there are many and varied stories that women have about the reasons they chose to have an abortion. The number

---

[24] https://www.Merriam-Webster.com.

alone—63,036,733—only tells how many abortions have been performed, but the truth is rarely told about the lives that we live and the one-sided propaganda that we listen to through popular music, movies, television, and all types of mass communication signaling us to believe that it is normal to engage in casual sex and that if a baby is conceived, then it's okay to use abortion as a birth control method. All of us can be swayed by what we see and hear in broadcast journalism and read in all types of written communication, including social media, in particular. For example, if terms like *fetus* and *embryo* are consistently used to describe what is growing inside our bodies, these words can create distance from the term *baby*. This one-sided propaganda from all forms of mass communication, including scientific research, makes way for young women not to have any feelings for what has been planted, or conceived, inside their bodies, and remorse for removing the fetus is minimal or nonexistent. The term *fetus*[25] means "baby" in Latin. However, using the word *fetus* can affect the thinking of millions of women to view abortion as acceptable birth control as well as serve the purpose of decreasing the population growth.

Do you think that propaganda is powerful enough to influence the minds of women to behave in a desired direction?

____

____

____

I would like to compare propaganda to what occurs in a petri dish. A petri dish is "a shallow circular dish with a loose-fitting cover used to culture bacteria or other microorganisms."[26] This definition uses the words *culture* and *growing bacteria* in a scientific sense. If the spread of propaganda substitutes growing bacteria as people introduce propaganda that a fetus is an insignificant blob of tissues to culture the bacteria, or people, then culture can produce thinking that

---

[25] https://www.dictionary.cambridge.org.
[26] https://www.AmericanHeritageDictionaryoftheEnglishLanguage.

has no concern for life, especially if the one-sided propaganda is continuously imported into the minds of people, particularly women. In this same petri dish, mass communication of propaganda stream into the minds of people that it is their right to destroy the lives within their bodies. Therefore, society is the petri dish.

Is it a right or an accommodation to have an abortion? What do you think?

What do you think would prevent a woman from viewing what is growing inside her body not as a fetus but as a growing baby from conception to live birth?

Continuous propaganda can manipulate or influence the way women think in a societal petri dish. Words can shield the truth that growing inside a woman's body is another human being called a baby, just like you were once inside your own mother's uterus, or womb.

This has been my experience. Through the years, I have heard so many women say the words "I am going to have a baby," and with further conversation, they will also tell me the due date. I can tell you that I have never heard a woman say that she was carrying a *fetus*. Of course, these announcements were always made when the woman didn't look pregnant, meaning her abdomen was not protruding outward with that baby-belly look. The term *fetus* is impersonal. It is designed to be. The words of choice for most women are "I'm going to have a baby" or "I'm pregnant." Anyone listening to her knows automatically that she is talking about having a baby. Terms like *fetus* are used to break down respect for the life of the unborn child and perpetuate decades of women not changing their sexual behaviors but instead preferring to cast the conceived unborn into a running tally of abortions performed.

Based on the number (63,036,733), it appears that being more selective in choices of men could reduce the number of abortions. Instead of an abortion, do you think that women could consider changing their sexual behaviors and interactions with men?

____

____

____

Asking these questions makes me think of a word in the dictionary, *morality*. *Merriam-Webster Dictionary* defines *morality* in part as rules of conduct pertaining to right and wrong.[27] I am asking you this question.

Do you think it is right or wrong to abort a baby or take pills to flush the remains down a toilet?

____

____

____

Do you think that this type of trauma is necessary in a woman's life?

____

____

____

How could a woman avoid these actions?

____

____

____

For example, I heard one pregnant woman say that she didn't know who the father was, so she decided to have an abortion. Another young woman said that she went out with this guy and that he bought her dinner, so she felt obligated to go to bed with him. She was going to have an abortion because she found out that she

---

[27] http://www.Merriam-Webster.com.

was pregnant. As I stated before, there are so many reasons women seek the accommodation of getting an abortion. An accommodation, according to *Merriam-Webster Dictionary*, is "something supplied for convenience or to satisfy a need: the providing of what is needed or desired for convenience."[28]

In what ways do you think that the circle of womanhood could lessen the number of abortions?

____

____

____

The one-sided propaganda that flourishes in society excludes the word *morals*.

Having sex is a private matter. Having sex is usually done in private between a male and female. Decisions about the creation of life should be made ahead of time between the people directly involved. Engaging in responsible sexual activity is the real choice between a man and a woman. It keeps all other outside parties out of your personal business.

Since sex is a private matter between a man and woman, why has it become so public that secular governments generally are involved in what happens in someone's bedroom?

____

____

____

However, if a girl does become pregnant because of rape or incest, laws have already been made since the 1950s to accommodate the tragedy and pain that such lawless sexual behaviors bring to those involved. It is also true that sometimes the young girl has the child. I have known of this happening, but the trauma initially caused a great deal of emotional upheaval and violence toward the rapist. People weigh these critical decisions differently.

---

[28] https://www.Merriam-Webster.com.

An age-old method exists, and it's called abstinence. Abstinence means not having sex. Many have practiced this method while concentrating on other areas of their lives, such as school, college, and beginning a career. If you decide to set that standard for yourself, then stick to it. A standard is what a criterion or judgment is based on. It is like drawing an invisible line about your conduct and stating with conviction that you will not cross over and violate your decision in this matter. Such high standards that we set for ourselves remain constant like the sun, the moon, the stars, and the beautiful rainbows that appear after a rain to remind us of God's covenant to humanity. We don't have to allow others to change our thinking about our sexual behaviors. I have known people who maintain their standards all the way to the marriage vow stated at their wedding ceremony.

Why do you think some women wait?

____

____

____

Do you see any value or benefit in a girl or woman not engaging in sexual experiences with different men?

____

____

____

Should a woman vet a man before allowing him to sit down and take root in her heart?

____

____

____

The term *vetting* is used in hiring practices. For example, when hiring a person for an important job, usually, a review is done concerning their background to evaluate their fit for that job, which can help the company select the right person. The reason is that the company makes an investment in their time and spends money to train that person. Vetting saves the company a great deal of time. At the beginning or the start date, they are interested in a person who they believe will be loyal and stay with them for years. It also allows the company to weed out other individuals who applied for the position but, if hired, would have proved to be a waste of time.

How does vetting compare to a woman looking for a lasting relationship?

____

____

____

Let's say we think they are handsome and have an appealing physique, and we like the sound of their laughter, among other things. They like the way we look. We feel the chemistry. We believe that we are off to a great start. However, we have to go past good looks and physical attraction and ask ourselves, "Who is this guy?" Start a questioning-and-observing process. Pay close attention to his behavior toward you and others. How does he talk? What things does he talk about? Do you agree with how he views life in general? Is he negative or positive about most things? How does he make you feel when you are around him? Is his mouth a cesspool of curse words constantly?

I have to tell you why I put the last question here. One day, I was in a grocery store, walking in a cross aisle, when I heard the voice of a small child say, "F———," only the child said the entire words. As I walked further and looked down the aisle, I saw that the child, a little boy about four or five years old, was saying that word to his mother. He was angry and disrespectful to his own mother. Words carry a spirit to them and, with that, a person's behavior.

Do you think there is a connection between the use of profane words and a person's behavior?

____

____

____

Does he smoke cigarettes, use marijuana, etc.? Does he get drunk? Is that okay with you?

____

____

____

What types of popular music does he listen to? Does he offer to let you listen to what you like if he is driving the car? Does he show tenderness toward you, like holding your hand or opening the door for you when entering a building? Ask him about his last girlfriend. What happened? Notice how he talks and his emotions concerning her. Has he been married before? What happened? You are not trying to find something to pick about this person, but you do want to evaluate his fit with you.

____

____

____

If you find things out about him that are objectionable to you, then don't ignore your female instincts or intuition. An analysis can save you a lot of time.

Since we are talking about a personal relationship, heartaches and pain with this individual would become nonexistent, and a decision to have an abortion would be eliminated.

In the circle of womanhood, we as women should see ourselves with real value. You have heard of the dollar or other currency being devalued, which means to lessen or downgrade its value. However, women don't lose their value if they know who they are and don't lose their identity.

A woman is innately prepared and capable of nurturing and caring for the previous, present, and future generations with seemingly boundless energy and authority. She is the perpetual appointee in eons of time—past, present, and future—and her value cannot be measured. Without a woman in this appointed position, there is no going forward of civilization with the existence of people. There is no going forward with continuous teaching or nurturing of the young without women. Therefore, a woman's value cannot be reduced. Even if a woman does not participate by adding to the existence of people, she still has great value. Her value can contribute to the flow of society in positive, immeasurable ways.

In what ways or areas do women make contributions in a society?

____

____

____

Unfortunately, women can devalue themselves by thinking negative thoughts about themselves. These thoughts can drag her self-perception down, as well as her self-confidence. Here is a partial list:

1. She has acne on her face.
2. She is overweight.
3. She doesn't think that she is pretty.
4. She didn't finish high school.
5. She dropped out of college.
6. She thinks that she is too skinny.
7. She has a child, and the man left her.
8. She has wrinkles.
9. She is bowlegged.

If a woman walks around with any devaluing thoughts about herself, she might not vet a man because she is just glad to have companionship for a while.

Should a woman stop being selective in her choice for companionship, a mate, or a husband just because of loneliness?

____

____

____

As a worthy member of value in the circle of womanhood, it should be our resolve to be true to our convictions. Don't yield or cast your convictions aside.

The truth is that women are born with confidence and beauty. We've gotten out of our mother's womb, and we are ready to rock and roll, excited to explore what is out there. Our eyes and ears, as well as all our other senses, are fully alert. We have confidence galore. I have never heard anyone say, "That's an ugly baby," so get it in your head that we are born beautiful. And then along comes the petri-dish effect that tells us through mass communication, both written and oral (like social media), and through other individuals we meet that something about ourselves is below standard. Then our confidence drops. We get an onslaught of advertisements that point out a woman's imperfections and how this or that product will improve our face, hair, body, teeth, you name it. Without being aware of how we have come to feel inside about ourselves, we may accept someone into our hearts for companionship, ignoring all red flags or warnings because of any of the above-listed reasons. Therefore, it is important to vet, vet, vet a future companion to minimize a decision to have an abortion.

Never forget to speak beautiful words about yourself. Stay confident.

It requires courage to not give in to peer pressure where someone wants you to act in a way that gets their approval. For example, other girls might tell you, "Everybody else is having sex, so why don't you?" This can happen in middle school, high school, and college. They may say that you are missing out, or boys might try to make you think and feel like you are such a little child if you refuse to have sex with them. Ignore them all. Stay strong. Be friends with those who support you and respect your goals. You are already a part of the dynamic circle of womanhood just by being born a female. You are also young, and that makes you a part of the next thinking generation (NTG).

My hope is that you will lionize the life of an unborn child. My hope is that you realize that we as living biological females are at the highest level of existence to think and reason logically about any topic. My hope is also that you will grow up knowing that you possess the willpower to maintain ownership over your own body. Try to make decisions by weighing the consequences ahead of time and take appropriate actions that will lead to your desired results in every area of your life.

I wish you the best life; therefore, I want you to know that I will always be your cheerleader!

Love,
Ms. Joyce

Here is a picture illustrating the three trimesters of pregnancy.

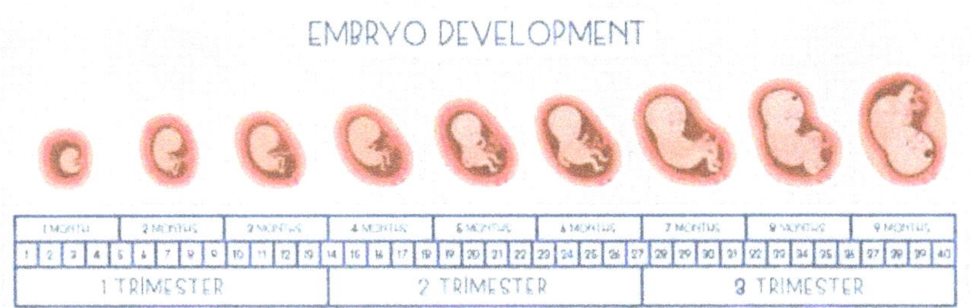

This is a picture showing the anatomy of a pregnant woman.

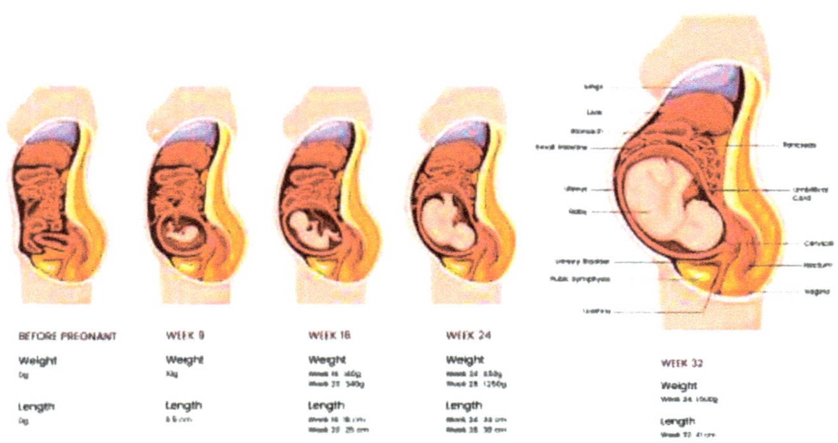

He has made
EVERYTHING
beautiful
IN ITS TIME
ECCLESIASTES 3:11

My name is Carolyn.

My name is Jaheem.

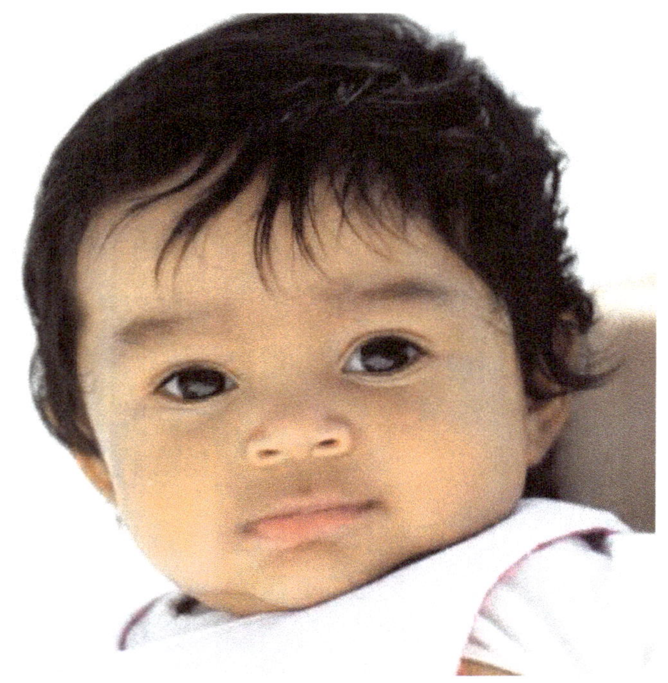

My name is Maria Isabella.

My name is Akito.

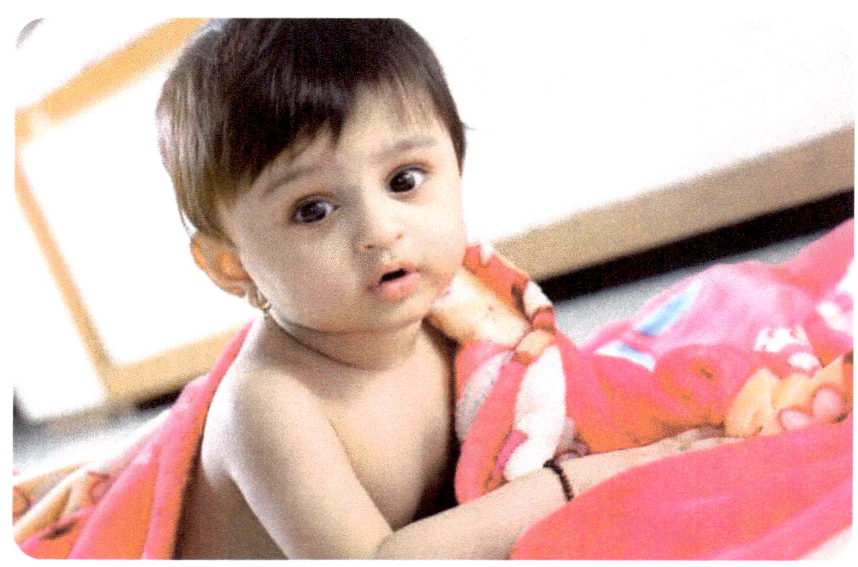

My name is Syed.

Bibliography

Cambridge Dictionary | English Dictionary, Translations & Thesaurus. Cambridge.org. 2019. http://dictionary.cambridge.org.

Center for Young Women's Health. 2019. https://youngwomenshealth. org/.Company, Houghton Mifflin Harcourt Publishing. n.d. "The American Heritage Dictionary Entry." Ahdictionary.com. http://ahdictionary.com.

English Dictionary, Thesaurus, & Grammar Help | Lexico.com. Lexico Dictionaries | English. 2019. http://lexico.com.

Languages.oup.com/Dictionaries/English-Language Learners. 2019. https://languages.oup.com/dictionaries/english-language-learners/.

Mayo Clinic. Review of "Healthy Lifestyle Pregnancy Week by Week." 2019. https://www.mayoclinic.org/healthy-lifestyle/pregnancy-week-by-week/basics/healthy-pregnancy/hlv-20049471. "MedlinePlus." Medlineplus.gov. 2019. http://medlineplus.gov.

Merriam-Webster Dictionary. 2019. https://www.merriam-webster.com/.

"Number of Abortions in US & Worldwide - Number of Abortions since 1973." n.d. Www.numberofabortions.com. http://numberofabortions.com.

ThoughtCo. 2019. https://www.thoughtco.com/

About the Author

Ms. Joyce taught middle school students and realized that teaching involved more than providing academic information. Sometimes students just wanted a listening ear or an encouraging confidence booster. This scenario happened to her on numerous occasions. However, she found that she didn't need to be in a school setting to be approached by a young person who wanted to talk to her. She 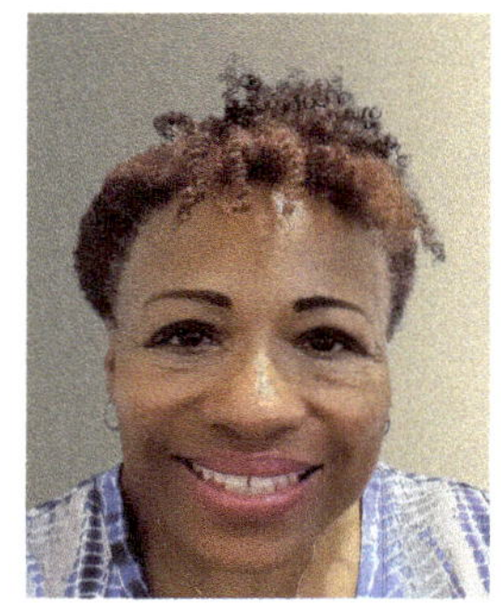 was in a store at a mall, and the salesclerk started helping her find a product but stopped and asked the author an unusual question: "If you were a younger you, what would you tell yourself now, thirty years later?" Ms. Joyce sensed that the salesclerk wanted to know about relationships. She proceeded to share some information about her own life, which prompted the salesclerk to say what was really on her mind. Before the conversation ended, the salesclerk had tears in her eyes as she thanked Ms. Joyce for her encouragement. They hugged, and Ms. Joyce left the store. She believes that this interactive journal came about as a result of her wanting to tell girls and young women everywhere that they are valuable and loved.